THE WHIRLING TOP

A Black Toymaker's Journey through

a Maze of Racism in America

LaMont Morris

Visit our website at **www.StillwaterPress.com** for more information.

First Stillwater River Publications Edition

Library of Congress Control Number: 2019920944

ISBN: 978-1-950339-68-6

1 2 3 4 5 6 7 8 9 10
Written by LaMont Morris.
Published by Stillwater River Publications, Pawtucket, RI, USA.

Publisher's Cataloging-In-Publication Data
(Prepared by The Donohue Group, Inc.)

Publisher's Cataloging-In-Publication Data
(Prepared by The Donohue Group, Inc.)

> Names: Morris, LaMont, author.
> Title: The whirling top : a Black toymaker's journey through a maze of racism in
>   America / LaMont Morris.
> Description: First Stillwater River Publications edition. | Pawtucket, RI, USA :
>   Stillwater River Publications, [2020]
> Identifiers: ISBN 9781950339686
> Subjects: LCSH: Morris, LaMont--Poetry. | African American artists--Social con-
>   ditions--Poetry. | Racism--United States--Poetry. | African Americans--Civil
>   rights--Poetry. | LCGFT: Poetry.
> Classification: LCC PS3613.O77375 W45 2020 | DDC 811/.6--dc23

This book is dedicated to

Marie

*The fire
that burned brightly
as the morning sun until
her loving flame
was no more.*

*The memory
of her fire remains alive and well;
her light will never grow dim within my
heart, soul and spirit.*

*The life
of love continues
as I am forever grateful
for the family of support from
my lovely wife*

Anne

and my daughter

Nabia

For me to love my fellow man
means that one's hatred for my skin
has no power over the soul
within me.

Contents

Preface

In the 1960's, I walked to and from school in the rain, the snow and in the heat of summer. After the ringing of the last school bells, I walked home and down the busy streets where the crossing guards blew their whistles letting us children know it was safe to cross. But, we as children were unaware that bigotry was steadily in motion, crossing racial lines in America and none of us received any signals of safe passage away from its racist history.

I am an American, and a professional artist, designer, toymaker, writer and inventor. All of the skin color labels that are placed on me can never define my true self and passion for life, liberty and the pursuit of happiness. I find that to understand the world around me I must peer through the disdainful lens of racism to see the angles, reflections, curves, distortions and contrasts that may interfere with my life and rights as an American citizen.

Writing poetry helps me to delineate life's, who, what, where and why of things. Being aware of my surroundings and the action-reactions of humanness is how I keep myself balanced against the forces of prejudice and its daily slights whether subtle and or overt.

The drawing on the front cover is an original self-portrait from the year 1980. It was drawn using black conte on 100% rag cotton paper. It holds meaning to me as my mother had a losing battle with cancer the same year the portrait was drawn. I cherish the memory of her love and deeply regret the injustices she had endured during the 1930s as a Negro girl. Though she was unable to speak as her condition worsened, she did however have a chance to see my artwork in her final days of life. When she saw the portrait, she looked at me with surprise and smiled. I felt her smile as, not assuring me, but one of, assuring herself that her young man will be just fine after she had left this world.

When I depict the human face in a drawing, or in any other medium, it requires close attention to what I see, guided by eye-hand coordination, an understanding of 3 dimensions and proportional considerations. I endeavor to capture an emotional image that appears to look back and interacts with the viewer as if it has life behind its eyes. Each ripple in the nose, lips, folds of skin were sketched as if connected to a being that is held together by flesh and bone beneath the light, shadows and curves in every line and stroke of black chalk on white cotton paper.

Thus, in this world, I am forced to view everything and everyone circumspectly. Looking in the mirror to draw my own face was the beginning of an artistic journey to retrace the ancient lines, curves, strength, tragedies, struggles and beauty that shaped the image of my parents and our forefathers in shadows and lighting as an insight to my future self.

1

WINDOWS

AND SEATS

Beautiful

It was beautiful
to be out and about
this weekend
with the glow of winter light
reflecting every curve of my face,
skin tone and curly head of hair,
while looking people straight
into their eyes
as an American man
that is proud
to be black.

Naturally

wherever i am
wherever i go
my face struts with me
black proud
and naturally
my facial expression
is my worldly possession
i wear it naturally
imagine me
rich or poor
walking through your door
imagine me as free
to be me
naturally

Lullaby

unknown white woman
shopping for a toy
for her little girl
and boy
we are in the same aisle
as i walk with a smile
i search and search
and there they are
the toys that emerged
from a dream
to the drawing board
and on to these shelves

a proud feeling indeed

again i see the unknown
white woman
adding to her cart
a toy i invented
she sees me looking at her
and the toys in her cart
we continue walking through the aisle
toward each other
but before we could pass each other
she clenches her purse
she had no clue of
the things i can do
if only for the joys
inside her cart is a quantum leap
that i could dream up the toys
that lull her children
to sleep

The Last First Black

Ever wonder who will be
the last first black
the one that is not under attack
where there is no need to score
nor mistreated whether rich or poor
the last task from a line of achievers
when others were disbelievers
climbed the last rung of the ladder
when race at last did not matter
the last lash to crack the ebony back
and break life's American barrier
of a red, white and blue ribbon
to become the awaited and
the last first black.

BLACK

BLACK
a word and a life
standing strong
like a pillar of dark energy in
the middle of forever
never dying in form or color
stretching a voice from sunrise
to sunset
a living breathing wide beauty
wrapped in the flavor
and proud face of heaven
black hot everyday
rain or shine
walking talking earth
and soil beyond the grip of the grave
yet ascending into the
midnight blackened universe where
a turbulent vortex of soul
lay painting every corner
of time

Window Seat

sweet black woman
loved that day
when she could pay
dust off the clay
ride and play
coins in a tray
where a transfer lay
whether sunny or gray
sit resting her feet
at a window seat
be on her way
downtown
her way
on a bus
without a fuss
where no
white man
or white woman
can say get up
remove your tired feet
and give me that seat

sweet black woman
loved that day
when she could pay
dust off the clay
sit resting her feet
at a window seat
ride and play
her way
with skin so beautiful
and brown
on a bus
headed downtown
pull the cord
to buzz her stop
near the stores
she'd often shop

Tender Headed

she reined in my
sweet young tender
headed hair caught
in tangles of my blackness
curled tightly
in stern words of
mama said wisdom
didn't i say no boy
sit cho ass down
you crying
i'll give you something
to cry about
roll your eyes at me
one more time
mama don't have time
for your mess
wait til your daddy
gets home

that boy is too big
for his britches
he so hard-headed
don't he know
hard heads
make soft behinds
life is hard son
mama loves you
but mama gonna
need you to pay
some attention
to what she say
and stop this
sassing me
all the time

Meridian Mississippi

down south
sun so hot
grandma and auntie
so happy
so glad
me sitting like a pee-wee
on their knee
sitting next to
or between them
on a big ass sofa
i jump down
they reach for me
their loose underarm skin
drooping and swaying
and both saying
"...come here boy
and give grandma
and auntie
some sugar.
lawd have mercy
that boy
sho tickles me."

African Soul

Black
Strength of mind
Roaring heart
A warriors royal soul
Blood
Bones of wisdom
Fighting spirit
African flesh boundless life

2
TENDERLY

Sketchbook

draw me
in your arms
posed in a still life
while there is
still life
pencil me in
retracing the first
rough sketches of our love
rendered and surrendered
in paper trails
with every line
and shadow
just as i
pictured us

Write Away

write a poem
that we can stuff
our life into

make it long enough
to hold me
and you

let it rhythm
and rhyme away
our time

let it rise
like the sun

hold it up
to the light

give it legs
that can run

and tuck us in
at night

Meet me Halfway

Meet me halfway
To the river,
Halfway between the
Ripples and the earth.

Meet me halfway
To the spirit,
Halfway between
Youth and my birth.

Meet me halfway
To the sun,
Halfway between
Yesterday and tomorrow.

Meet me halfway
To the soul,
Halfway between the
Laughter and the sorrow.

Cloaked

we bundle our skin
like two seasons in timelessness
watching the shadows
spin around us
at the speed of soulfulness
as blue as
the winter sky
cloaked in summers
humid morning dew
we stand frozen
by the rays
of every sunrise
and sunset
in our life

Flaming Chapters

Of all the pages
I've written,
I've only shared
with you
the sweet words,
the ones that I write
when I need to
escape the fire
of my own troubles.

I'm not trying
to be dishonest
but I didn't want
those flaming chapters,
to trouble you.
I didn't want
my fires
to burn you, too.

3

PORTRAIT
OF A SOUL

Action And Figures

My father figures
were real figures
of action.

I recall
the many dark nights
I was tucked safe and sound
into bed by a black
living breathing
male figure of action
that saved the day
and saw me through
stormy times and strife.

A man
not made of plastic.

A man
that could bend
and not break
under the pressures of life.

Sense of Smell

My sense of smell is a cynical
force that can polarize
the magnetic waves
that hold my dreams together tightly
between every black and grey strand
of my curly head of hair.

I'm black enough to love my fellow man
enough to see that hatred rots from
the head and has no power over
the sweet and fragrant soul
within me.

Hair thickly and coarse is my guardian,
judge and jury to my quiet gravity
in peaceful protest
combed out in a fist raised afro
demonstrating my golden blackness
into perpetuity
right on down to the root
without an air of cynicism
that black is beautiful.

Crazy

with you so crazy
i don't have to know the words
to say the words

with you so crazy
i don't have to touch you
to feel you

you are the kind of crazy
i dream about

you are the kind of insanity
that opened my mind

American Artist

He was a master painter
an unknown abstract artist in warm flesh
splashing his manhood on canvases
stretched across the framework of the
Jim Crow gallery of reds, whites and blues.

An ingenious use of his medium and color
palette would create a beautiful family portrait.

He endured a past sketched in lines of inequality.
His freedom of expression received harsh critiques.

"We Don't Serve Negroes Here"

Sometimes his color palette consisted of:

"Whites Only,"

other times,

"Colored Only."

Yet, he was among the many that were reinventing
humanity one Negro child at a time, while painting
a spectrum of a life worth living.

Complexion

Turbulent stars
whirling my world
ignite the light
of my thirsty soul.
My face waves a smile
at the universe
in a complexion
known for drawing
unwelcome attention
in denial of the might
and powerful ancestry
within my galaxy.

Attention Shoppers!!!

It seems
so simple to
shop while black
and just take my time
casually
looking around
in the department store
for a holiday gift
for my wife.

Though
respect is an assumption
I dare not make
and feeling secure
is a risk
I can not take.

To be sure
let me ask
the guy that keeps
following me around
in the store
where I might find
the regular or
extra crispy cameras
profiling and
monitoring
my every move.

Intersection

There is not found a soft soothing
whimsical path that intersects my
favorite childhood toy side-by-side
the daily diet of racism my parents
were served and forced to swallow.

My life was greener than a freshly
cut lawn leaking its fragrance into
the air with just one exhale of breath
from heaven reaching into every
pore of my God given body and soul.

I played with those that were playing,
lived with those that were living,
laughed with those that were laughing,
learned from those that were dying,
cried with those that were crying.

I cupped my parent's tears in my hands
to bathe in their sorrows, their history,
making sure the drops hadn't touched
the ground until my skin was emphatic
enough to intersect with any man.

4

PERSISTENCE
OF WONDER

Beloved Family Man

i can only imagine

the precious moments
he'd live
feeding his family
and all he could give
some days laughed
some days cried
sat and enjoyed
watching his children
with pride

i can only imagine

on Christmas day
his children opening gifts
and watching them play
some combing the hair
of a favorite doll
cleared for takeoff a toy plane
created words using
only one vowel
switched the lever to
an electric train
from tricycles to bicycles
guiding their play
from snowballs to icicles
on a winter's day

i can only imagine

he took out time for family fun
all before their day was done
playing piano with many songs to sing
this beloved family man
Dr. Martin Luther King

Colorblind Rainbows

Children are colorblind rainbows
when no one is looking.
Innocent smiles are true
embracing innocently every hue.

Children are the keepers of stars
and masters of bedtime moonlight
inhaling and exhaling
the sweet smell of infinity
through the night.

Zigzagging

in 1964 our coloring together
was like sharing
in a special community
with kids who were trying
to figure themselves out
on paper
in the zigzag
hyperbolic world
around them
whether drawn
as stick figures
or as symbols
that represent
the sun and stars
a shiny rainbow
and crescent moons
it boiled down to shapes
and lines in the language
of an uncorrupted composition
it felt like we were all drawing
our own diagram
to a world of fun
and only the artist
could best decipher
from their map
where the fun could be found

JOY

it's quite a
joy
to see
a child
with a
toy

with reeds
and the bellows
it whistles
and zooms
with a sound
of joy
that fills
a room

inventing
a toy
is quite
a joy

Floatation

The playground held all their secret treasures
to swing and climb on with laugh out loud
merry-go-rounds whirling energy deeper than
the darkest winding lagoon.

And the rising sun wiped the rain and clouds
from their cheeks and covered their eyes
from the rays of every tortured rainbow
under the moon.

Just children floating along the saccharine bursts
from pink bazookas playing and discovering
that they are greater than any toy surprise
and lighter than any balloon.

Seas of Wonder

upon the face so crystal and shy
children play in brimming seas of wonder
lovely breeze where the trees sway and kites fly
bearing dreams that scream louder than thunder

let's tumble and toss in the summer sun
setting us free to laugh hop skip and jump
enjoy this season til our days are done
seeds of ripe falling apples after the thump

Flying Bedroom

a toy
lovely dream
a child at play
eyes wide opening
mysteries surreal
flying bedrooms
toys on the shelf
emerge from the sea
innocence whimsical
touching discovering
every caricature
of reality

Plastic Day

an elastic
plastic day
teeter-tottering
with a funhouse mirror
of dreams
skipping hopping leapfrogging
and laughing away
the heat wave of summer
between each sip
of lemonade
my mama made

Hurling and Whirling

Wherever a toy appeared
a tension was created,
the tension of, imagination.
Sometimes for a season
as a flame
burning brighter
than a summer sun.
Or as ice cold
and frozen in time.
Holding a toy for hours
in the palm of my hand
had held its grip on me
and held me longer and tighter.
And somehow I knew that a toy
would always send me hurling
and whirling on a rollercoaster ride
from, Eureka,
to, back to the drawing board,
to, Eureka...

Idea

Talk with the fun
Tickle the morning light
Dance with the sun
Smile higher than a kite

Dreaming up oceans
Traverse the breeze
Ideas and potions
Draw me in with ease

The Sandbox

How can one create fun
without ever discovering fun
or engaging in it on a regular basis?
How can one coax a child to smile
without knowing of innocence and childhood
and dreams without rules complete with
never ending merriment?
It is about learning
through the language of my smiles
on the playground mingling
with their smiles,
the time between spaces,
the spaces between time,
discovering what is
round and round,
over and under
and upside down.
How can one invent amusement
without ever being amused as a child?
How can one begin to conceive of fun
without playing with other children
and childhood friends?
Just open up that big fat jar of
kid stuff and immerse in it.
It is a rollercoaster journey through
miles and miles of smiles
on swings; smiles on skates,
smiles on bikes, smiles on wagons,
smiles that bat and bounce a ball,
and hands that play catch.

It defies gravity in leapfrogs,
hops, skips and jumps.
Smiles can be found in a blade of grass,
a drop of water in a pond
and fingers sifting sand from the sandbox.
How can one create fun without recognizing
that innocent smiles are beams of light
that can melt the heart and mold it
into time well spent and a life worth living?
Smiles are timeless, limitless, and free,
without rules, race, or ethnicity.

Toy Box

Wit and whimsy
Wind-up gizmo
Collecting frenzy
Pocket yo-yo
Fun to remember
Childhood pleasures
Toys in December
And antique treasures

The One Hair

When I create a marketable plaything I don't see the soft
glow of innocence in a child nor lose myself in the toy land
of pure fantasy.

I see T's crossing I's dotted steeped in research
and development and guarding my conscience away
from entering a stream of ugliness.
Always doing due diligence and justice by design
enough to navigate clear of Murphy's law.

Still I see in permutation and tragic scenarios
the crying faces of children
the pissed off
the dreaded
and futile reaching out to a parent or guardian
of an injured child and expressing true empathy
yet with nothing to dry their tears

I feel pain, sorrows and disappointment and a loss of trust
by a design flaw as the instigator of hurt and mourning.
I see the shit hitting hard the fan in slow motion replayed over
and over into syndication.
I see angry white fingers pointing straight at my black skin and
feel the searing heat of molten lava I'm barely breathing choking
on the smoke of getting burned on an assignment.
I see the sleepless nights as the never-land never again land
and the first dream of my worst nightmare perhaps caused by
the simplest of miscalculations all because I'd be the man
responsible for the one hair harmed on a child.
Thank God that I was never the engineer on that train
of tears.

5
THIS
SIDE UP

Baggage

A little baggage
a long way to go
you carry the tunes
while I hold the kisses
you hold the memories
while I keep the faith

Let's unpack
unfold
sort out
our differences
and try each other on
for size

Take out that smile
you used to wear
and put it on again
I'll unzip the laughter
let it linger in the air
brightly like a sunrise

Atop Eggshells White

He walked
at his own pace
atop eggshells
at every corner
and every place.

On eggshells white
like the privilege
crackling below his
black feet
he walked,
he heard the talk
but kept walking
at his own beat.

Now he's too old
with years of tears
to run away and
tip-toe around
men's privileged fears
or try to erase
and comfort the
boiling point look
on their face.

Pedestrians

and perchance
i yield to you
a right of passage
as i walk
while black

it's not because
of anything i've
gained or lack

you just had an
encounter with
an altruistic
darkly hued
gentleman
with manners
and tact

Bouncing Ball

coin in the slot
pull the rod while it's hot
follow the bouncing ball
steel ball cold rolling
street signs glowing
swivel to the left
bump it to the right
down an alley
spinning off the walls
straight down the hole
up and down the hole
all night
like lightening
until it pops

Reverse Engineer

Like a key in the back
of a tin toy soldier
her disparaging words would
wind me up
again and again.
She was my teacher
and the mother of this invention.
Somehow I managed
to keep walking straight and tall,
though un-amused.
When she opened her
toy box of slights
she knew that I would be there
to play with and that I would be
standing at attention.
All the while I wondered
where in her diorama of insults
would I be standing the next time
my emotions
have to do battle
with her newfound amusement?

Rather Be

Rather suffer the hate for skin
darkened by the African sun than to
be servile to the hater

Rather be loved by those in a room
that is lesser than to check one drop
of dignity in a room that is greater

Rather shoulder the weight of
disappointments than to be beholden
to the fear of failure

Rather hold the yardstick with a right
to an opinion than to the golden rules
by another man's measure

Rain of Ecstasy

The rain of ecstasy
Rises and falls.

The thunder rumbles
And louder it calls.

The clouds are breaking
But not my will.

Storm of passion
Hold me still.

6

LOVE, LIGHT, AND SHADOW

After

after the writing is done
who will read

after the paint dries on the canvas
who will see

after the clay is cast
who will touch

after the flesh returns to dust
who will know

Dressed in Dreams

as usual
all dressed up
this morning in skin
born the color
of midnight
ready to start
my day with
the sunshine
of my life
until the stars
undress us
as dreamers
embracing the moon
as our pillow

Out of the Clear Blue

I am pleasantly dwarfed by the blue sky
And humbled by its stately persistence.
Even when my life seems to go awry
The encroaching blue is my providence.
Out of the clear blue, a dreamer escapes
And lifts me with ease, higher and higher.
Cerulean skies dignify the landscape
As the rising sun explodes its fire.
Whispering white patches, drifting along,
While the ocean reflects the blue yonder.
Birds fly freely—filling the void with song,
With awestruck pause, a moment to ponder.
So long as the azure bathes in suspense
So long will the sky overwhelm my sense.

Ocean Air

at times i'm surrounded by people that fear
being surrounded by me

ever wonder if the ocean
air feels differently
on skin that's

straight
gay
black
Indian
latino
white
asian

ever feel
that what
others fear
and say
is truly
unimportant
and a waste
of your time
and by dawn
that the only thing
that truly defines us
is the air we breathe
and how passionate we are for life

Personal Space

the sun cautiously
raised its head
wide eyed and curious
for a moment
like the head of a turtle
slowly emerging
from its shell
and back again

that's too bad
because she was never
a morning person
yet the morning sun
could smooth out her edges
and soften the burrs
that rise like goose bumps
down her spine
and warm the moist skin
of her cold shoulders
before the caffeine aroma
rang pungent and sweetly
beckoning the first
deep steamy sip
of her morning brew

after her second cup
she had the space
and time to thaw
but for now
i tucked my head
back into its shell
devoid of curiosity
for the moment
until the second pot
begins to brew
then i'll
take mine black

Seasons

the ocean
is my mother
pregnant with life

the sun
is my father
providing ultraviolet sperm

and i am
a season
living and changing
day by day

Potion

they stood there
spilling the last drop
of their love potion

not even poetry
could set them back
into motion

that last drop
dissolving without tears
or emotion

7

PUSH
AND PULL

Whimsical Machine

you'd love to
push me pull me
around like a toy

take me here
and there for your
pleasure your joy

your personal
whimsical machine
going your way

with me tucked
neatly in your pocket
ready to play

Quizzical

When a white woman
clenches her purse
in the toy aisle
as I approach
it is the most
unusual sensation
of ecstasy
and reproach.

The anomaly of me
an African-American
toymaker
comes face-to-face
with an antiquated
distain for
my blackness
sharing this narrow
quizzical space.

The Court of Public Opinion
(Race and Tragedy)

A white female gasps for air, "I can't breathe,"
while in a struggle resisting arrest
from 4 black female officers whom believe
it's their sworn duty to sit on her chest.

That one black female officer had applied
an illegal chokehold on the white female.
She exhaled her final breath then she died.
Every attempt to save her life would fail.

Would the scale of justice be equally balanced
when the court of public opinion is well rehearsed,
or tip to one side and go un-challenged,
when race and tragedy are reversed?

The Whirling Top

I've witnessed
the great spin of racism
swirling and whirling
like a top
with destructive demolition
of democracy force
destroying in its path human rights
freedom of speech, thought
and liberties
as its momentum goes
bouncing and bashing
unwavering
steady as she goes
without a wobble
in and out
every corner of American life.

Self-Respecting Face

My brother, my dawg, we're cowboys and black
and black enough to have each other's back.

You slapped me in my self-respecting face
while you sang the N-word in our workplace.

Just trying to rise like any old man
while refusing to wear the white man's brand.

Don't chain us to failure then throw away the key
into echo chambers beneath our dignity.

My brother, my dawg, we're cowboys and black
and black enough to have each other's back.

Respect yourself enough to remain hired
cuz, singing the N-word will get you fired.

No Bell Rang

When that bell rang
you knew
school was out.
Nothing like sailing through
those double doors
on Friday
or on the start of
summer vacation.
But no bell rings
for the end of racism
no double doors to exit
no summer break
or vacation
from being the
unwitting student
chained to learning
the many forms
of its bigotry.
Whether you are
a young black child
or a successful black man
or black woman
no bell rang
to signal
that finally
there was
justice for all.

Don't Ask

Don't ask why
the black man struggles
to get by.

Don't ask why
he takes an eye
for an eye.

Don't ask why
his hopes are sweet
by and by.

Don't ask why
he lives to
laugh and cry.

Don't ask why
he learned to swallow
the big lie.

Don't ask why
he spreads his wings
to fly.

8

HUMAN CARGO

American Heroes

hand me
your heroic lives
and overlook the fringed
edges of rivers
that chain your blackness
to motionless memories
slaughtered by lies
buried in graves
beneath the feet
and sound of men
bidding at the final bell
raising the price
of owning
the negro

Indelible

night air drags
an ancient stone mystery
flint and fire
burn my flesh into ash
i can smell
the scent of our history
smoldering with each
indelible lash

Lynching Of A Negro

Weakness finds the strength to kill the innocent
Hate is devoid of love caught in a web of lies
Binding what is true for the sake of argument
For the honest soul in a man never dies

The fear of a man is the object of his death
Though the dreams he had remain forever
Loved ones sorrows are echoed in their breath
With a history you can't strangle or sever

Human cargo of Negro people to beat and batter
In single file move closer to the final drum
Killed by those that think only their lives matter
Before dying hums a low hum their day will come

1ˢᵗ Amendment Timeout Called

Amid the gleam, screams and roar of crowded NFL
Stadiums, shoulder-padded giants of men are found
kneeling atop the manicured green and chalk white
yard lines until justice remains inbound.

Athletes kneeling at the National Anthem harkened
back to all the years their forefathers were enslaved.
They know the "Star Spangled Banner" was not penned
for the Negro nor were its banners meant to wave.

The lyric is a reminder to every soul to never forget
the shame and misery of slavery's degradation.
The American players quietly kneel, watch and wait
in peace hoping for equality in this Nation.

Why, because black men are brutalized by those
charged with serving and protecting and still they fall.
Profane words had arisen calling their mothers a bitch
for seeking the men in blue to help them pass this wall.

They kneel in the shadows with like-minded men
that brave the injury of injustice to their democracy.
While the flaming torch of liberty is striped away from
their grip they refuse to stand for such hypocrisy.

An official timeout is called on their freedom as citizens,
in search of the penalty for kneeling on the playing field.
Their 1st Amendment rights are intentionally grounded
where their protest will remain and never yield.

Affirm

Is he unpatriotic
because he acknowledged
his enslaved descendants
more than standing
for an anthem
that never stood for him
and his ancestors freedom?

Or is he more patriotic
because the world can
clearly affirm
the history
of the real America
that was built
on the flesh
and bloodied backs
of the Negro?

Soul Piercing

today i hear
the voice of prejudice
loud and clearly
but louder still is the
unimaginable
soul piercing clink
in every link
that chained
my African ancestors
to fates
and destinies of
lost lives
lost fortunes
the sound of poverty
the sound of racism
the loud and
the deafening silence
of the betrayal
of generations

Parading Around

unlike some
i don't
have the privilege
of listening to
the sweet sound of
saying nothing
amid a bigoted
repeat of history
and its embrace
of sweet slumber
of doing nothing
and never changing
never removing the
sting of inhumanity
then live life
with open eyes
parading around
like it was
only a dream

Aboard

long ago
we were
not passengers aboard
massive ships with
privileged accommodations

we were in fact
its enslaved cargo
with no right
of passage
but served only as
the human tools
to build America's
land of the free

Cargo

along oceans waves
rising black and macabre
tossing tuning regrets
the African elephant
remembers the dreadful
regrettable bloodied
dreams it can never forget

human cargo of hurt
shackled union sailing
dark waters of fear
sudden lives interrupted
in hellish force kill
the one divine tear

Eyes White Privileged

eyes white privileged
shut tight and dry
by slavery's bloody tears
and black history's years
never blinking
batting not an eye
enough to cry
only to see
their lives die

Against Eternal Twilight

a time
living in borrowed flesh
stands
panic stricken without adrenaline
coursing through its veins
where time
not honored lives
buries an ocean of tears
mingled between air and soil
and the bones of
huddled masses
in the black of night
the black of earth and sky
of lost dreams
against eternal twilight
that found
souls awakening

9

BELLS, WHISTLES, AND FRAGILE BEAUTY

Slingshot

The fastest way
to reach you
was to use
the slipstream
of your soul
as a slingshot
til I could get close enough
to tether my love
tightly around your
heart.

Her Shadow

her shadow clings
to the wall
i lick it to the bone
silhouette and all

my lips and tongue
play shadow puppet
picking her clean
licking joyfully
obscene
until nothing
is left on that wall
except
the rising sunrays
of morning light

Just for You

I can't sing
I can't dance
I can't play basketball

All that I can do
is love

My love sings
My love dances
My love is athletic

My love is a skill
that I perform
just for you

The Traveler

I didn't know those tall
hide and go seek
treed backyards existed
which employed
an invisible Cicada
and a dragonfly
whose name
escapes me.

Yet, its residents
were kind enough
to welcome me
as a traveler
on a first class journey
to run and play through the
gentle breeze where
heaven on earth
covered its face
counts to ten,
and sings
…come out, come out
wherever you are…
never peeking
before opening its eyes
to come
searching for me.

Drum Skin Rhythm

i would like to think
that i have a
good heart
so forgive me
for not letting you
interrupt it
and arrest
its black
warm-temperate
african
tight as a
drum skin rhythm
with your blues

10

OBSESSION

Dragons

an anger
hot like the breath of
dragons
breathes enough fire to
heat our discussion
hot and airy blazing furnace
of hot tempered words
consuming all the oxygen
in the room
and suffocate
every reason to be
speaking to each other
at all

Vigilante

He looked beyond the thunder,
At men that rage and plunder.

Where peace is scarce and fleeting,
And sounds from hearts were beating.

And women whom lack escape
From the hands that force her rape.

Their crimes had made him wonder
How he could put them under.

Hate

Her beautiful
black flesh
refused to crawl
when hate
walked through
the door.

Hate was
dead to her
as if it didn't
exist anymore.

The Dozens

Words whiz by,
They whiz by fast.
They'll poke you in the eye—
Bite you in the ass.

Talk about'cha mama,
Yo grandma' too.
Stirr'n much drama,
And aim'n at you.

Oh she's quite a wit
And always a hit.
Just be careful where you sit
When she talks that shit.

Reprisal

A night
of sabotage clings
neatly
against tomorrow's dish
served best cold
amidst
ruthless taste buds

After midnight
our lives
will never again
be on the menu
of men
with an appetite
for cruelty
and violence

Jealousy

I've tried to run faster
than jealousy.
I've tried to stay ahead
in the race.
I can't seem to move past
the suspicion,
nor
continue running at this
jealous pace.

Roaming Eyes

from his home
in Macon Georgia
he wrote it all down
at night
alone
in privacy
unedited
safe and sound
from roaming eyes
he scripted
all of his own
thoughts
when white folks
aren't looking at
his plans
schemes and
new formulas
for living and being
the black man
he always imagined
himself to be

Jump Ball

a jump ball
of a day
between the cops
and a man
driving while black
now with his hands up
in the air
desperately searching
for the...innocent
till proven guilty...dexterity
that will elevate him
high enough
to tap the ball
in his court
and save
his own life
in this game
in overtime

Siren in the Night

a siren
in the night
relentlessly
weeping
wailing
and crying for some
official attention
to pull-over
an unarmed
black man
driving his
black shiny rover
maybe he had
"the talk"
home training
from his father
who schooled him about
driving while black and
unlawful enforcement
or he's all together destined
to be face down
on the ground
while his family
weeps
wails
and cries for
their loved one
at another senseless
bout with
police brutality
aired on
the evening news

11
PAST TENSE

Good Friends

I've got
a hand full of
good friends.

Folks to talk to,
clown around with
shoot the breeze,
compare notes and debate
unimportant issues.

People to
check myself against
to stay balanced.

Folks that know where my
hot buttons are,
but would
never press them.

Friends that don't leave my ass
in the cold when my business
is hot and boiling
in the streets.

Sisters and Brothers
that gave a damn
and still give a damn
when no one else would.

I Didn't Have To Be A White Boy

I didn't have to be a white boy
to watch a Monarch butterfly
sip sweet nectar from a flower.

I didn't have to be a white boy
to chase a firefly below the
stars until the midnight hour.

I didn't have to be a white boy
to walk along the beach
collecting seashells by the shore.

I didn't have to be a white boy
to visualize the world in perspective
and sketch it like none before.

I didn't have to be a white man
to create new and unique playthings
that brings smiles to girls and boys.

I didn't have to be a white man
to lay my head down at night
to dream up those toys.

Let's Go Outside

a free spirit
curiosity inventiveness
the usual
nicks scrapes and splinters
pushing and shoving
popping wheelies on my bike
hide & go seek
blowing bubbles
hopping skipping
flying kites
paper airplanes
kick ball dodge ball
hopscotch
playing catch
snowball fights
make a snowman
running and sliding
on the ice in my sneakers
emotions and inner self
giggling side by side
with my sense of balance
coordination dexterity
a story-land shared by white black
and children of color globally
that didn't have to be rich
to be curious or inventive
a universal freedom
to all kids that recognized
the 3 words
tag you're it

Wishful Dreams

Our full moon
is drunk with the sadness
of guilty
and forgotten
sleepless nights
where the ship
has sailed
and there is no stopping
the train
that left the station.

The clouds
are rolling in now
just in time
to douse the light
of the moon
and sober up all our dark
and dusty
wishful dreams.

Bag of Chips

today was
one of those days
that had burst opened like a
salty potato chip bag of tricks
with everyone wanting a bite
crunching away every bit of
starch within me
savoring the last licks
until there was nothing left
but a foiled
crumpled greasy bag
of grime deflated
by a humiliating
waste of time

12

BLACK
WATER

Black Water

you were out witted today
and beaten at your own game
though you look at me
as not the victor
but as the one who
should be damp with shame
but when it rains it pours
and you'll need a set of oars

revenge in your eyes
i find as no surprise
didn't you know that
water is wet
and downpours
lead to floods

your loss
was more than losing to me
because i was once
a ripple on your river
but now
i am a roaring
raging sea

Gears of Intolerance

A life of
hurling and whirling
living amidst
the gears of intolerance
where my professionalism
remains firm and creative.
I use all the playful
bells and whistles
of toy design
that bring smiles
to the young and old
despite the persistence
of bigotry
spinning all around my
blackness.

Visions In Blackness And Blue

I see with a
selfish eye
handed down
in pitch-blackness.

I see
shadows of men
who once stood
in the light of
my great grandfather,
men that have
quietly
come to rest
comfortably below
my tired black feet.

The wind blows
along the shore
and the dust
from dead black men
whirl as restless visions
in blackness
and blue.

Enough To See

I'm black
and enough
to love myself
enough to see
that hatred
has no power
over the soul
within me.

Evolutions

I felt her vexation
from every lick of the lash
the sting in her spare the rod
spoil the child beliefs in the long
belt straps and freshly picked switches
the same way the white folks
were lashing out at her image and spirit.

I felt her long history
of giving in and giving up in her hellish-bent
for corporal punishments through a disdainful lens
"...well, momma whipped us good fashion
and her momma whipped her
and her mamma's master
whipped all his niggers and so it goes."
So boy, take your medicine like a man.

I felt the change in her heart
as she listened from the turntable the
soulful sounds of black and beautiful music
whirling its way through the civil rights movement.

I felt her sense of newly found confidence
as we boarded a bus on the way downtown
and letting me sit at the window seat
near the front.

I felt her moment of satisfaction
when she told me that after standing in long lines
days before Christmas that she had
carted the last popular toy on the shelf
a few moments before a white woman.
All she knew was that it was on my Santa's list.

I felt her evolving and blooming like a rose
amid the thorns of racial intolerance.

I felt the sorrow in her eyes
for ever lashing out at me
whether physically or in harshness of voice.

To Just Be

I've been pushed
and pulled
all week at work
though in a
good way
but TGIF

I'll need
a dark
and sweeter than
chocolate reason
stronger than
wetting my whistle
on my morning
black coffee
to get up
and give up
my time
to just be

if only for a moment

LaMont Morris in 1997

About the Author

LaMont Morris worked for 25 plus years in the toy industry as a Product Design Manager, Sr. Advanced Concepts Designer, and Future Now Lead Industrial Designer. He holds several patents independently and with co-inventors. He has developed numerous award-winning toys that achieved market success.

After graduating in 1985 from The Cleveland Institute of Art with a BFA in Industrial Design, he was hired by Marvin Glass & Associates, the acclaimed toy invention firm in Chicago that invented classic toys and games such as Mouse Trap, Simon, Rock em Sock em Robots, Lite-Brite and more. In 1988, the Hasbro Playskool Division hired him and now his design effort and teamwork result in toys that entertain, inspire and educate children around the world.

In 1991 a new G.I. Joe: A Real American Hero action figure was created by using Morris's name and the sculpted likeness of Morris and featured in Action Figure Digest Magazine for the now popular African-American G.I. Joe character "Heavy Duty." Heavy Duty was featured in the G.I. Joe comics published by Marvel Comics and in the G.I. Joe: Spy Troops CGI animated film.

In 1994 the Hasbro Children's Foundation commissioned Morris to create works of art as awards to honor the late News Anchor Peter Jennings and the Staff at ABC News for their contributions to children's news coverage around the world. In 1997 Morris was again commissioned by Hasbro's Corporate Communications Group to do works of art for their newly renovated World Headquarters. His creativity was exhibited along with other Rhode Island artists and craftsman at the opening of the Hasbro Children's Hospital, and as a fund raising effort for the Women & Infants Hospital. Morris was also commissioned by the Walt Disney Studios to do works of art for their "Fab-Five" characters.

Through teamwork he received two Playskool Research & Development Product Awards in 1993. Child Magazine's: Best Toy of 96. Parents Magazine: Top Toy of 97, as one of the new products, which helped increase Playskool's Market Share in the Infant Toy category. The Toy Industry Association 2001 Best-Licensed Preschool Toy of the Year (T.OT.Y.). Parenting Magazine, Nick Jr. Magazine and Child Magazine Best Toy of 2003.

He is also featured in the Hasbro, Inc. "Come Play With Us" DVD and he appears on the Hasbro, Inc. Careers Website as part of a Global Public Relations recruitment initiative. Morris has served on the Hasbro Diversity Committee to help recommend ways to retain "people of color" and to identify ways to include minority representation at all levels within the organization including its Rhode Island World Headquarters.

In 2005 he was featured in Black Enterprise Magazine (Excellence in Design) as one of America's Top Black Designers. Morris is a member of the Washington, DC Chapter of the Organization of Black Designers. In 2006 the Institute of Black Invention and Technology featured him as, Inventor of the Month and includes his work as part of a traveling Museum. Morris has contributed to innovations to the classic toy Easy-Bake Real Meal Oven, (2003) which includes a heating element that safely and efficiently replaced the lightbulb, and in 2006 the Easy-Bake Oven was inducted into the National Toy Hall of Fame.

In 2007 he was one of the honorees at the Chicago Museum of Science and Industry in an Industrial Design exhibit entitled, "Designs for Life" and as part of their Black Creativity Program. The goal of the Museum in mounting this exhibition was to inspire young people, particularly from the African-American community, to pursue careers in Industrial Design. During Black History month 60,000 visitors to the Museum were anticipated to view the exhibit. Morris was recently elected as a new member to the Rhode Island Black Heritage Society's Board of Directors.

(12) **United States Design Patent** (10) Patent No.: **US D486,533 S**

Morris (45) **Date of Patent:** ** **Feb. 10, 2004**

(54) **TOY OVEN**

(75) Inventor: **LaMont Curtis Morris**, Hope, RI (US)

(73) Assignee: **Hasbro, Inc.**, Pawtucket, RI (US)

(**) Term: **14 Years**

(21) Appl. No.: **29/182,261**

(22) Filed: **May 22, 2003**

(51) **LOC (7) Cl.** **21-01**
(52) **U.S. Cl.** **D21/542**
(58) **Field of Search** D21/483, 523–525;
D7/350.4, 350.1; 446/481, 479; 219/413,
386, 405

(56) **References Cited**

U.S. PATENT DOCUMENTS

4,249,067	A	*	2/1981	Cummings	.... 219/405
D260,104	S	*	8/1981	Klawitter	.... D21/524
4,563,573	A		1/1986	Hartelius et al.	
4,781,646	A	*	11/1988	Dibley	.... 446/481
5,422,458	A		6/1995	Simmel	
5,451,745	A	*	9/1995	Goldberg et al.	.... 219/413

5,528,014	A	*	6/1996	Goldberg et al.	.... 219/386
D372,058	S	*	7/1996	Yang	.... D7/350.4
6,033,286	A	*	3/2000	Langlinais	.... 446/481
6,509,550	B1		1/2003	Li	
D473,600	S	*	4/2003	Khasminsky	.... D21/524
D475,236	S	*	6/2003	Lai	.... D7/350.1

* cited by examiner

Primary Examiner—Raphael Barkai
(74) Attorney, Agent, or Firm—Michael Best & Friedrich LLP

(57) **CLAIM**

The ornamental design for a toy oven, as shown.

DESCRIPTION

FIG. **1** is a perspective view of a toy oven;
FIG. **2** is a front elevational view thereof;
FIG. **3** is a top plan view thereof;
FIG. **4** is a rear elevational view thereof;
FIG. **5** is a right side elevational view thereof;
FIG. **6** is a left side elevational view thereof; and,
FIG. **7** is a bottom plan view thereof.

1 Claim, 4 Drawing Sheets

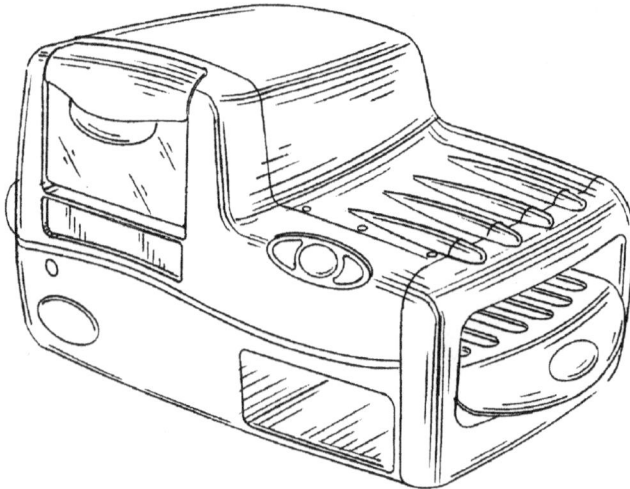

(12) **United States Patent** (10) **Patent No.:** **US 7,914,361 B1**
Morris et al. (45) **Date of Patent:** **Mar. 29, 2011**

(54) **ENTERTAINMENT APPARATUS AND METHODS PROPELLING TOY VEHICLES ABOUT MULTIPLE TRACKS**

(75) Inventors: **LaMont Morris**, Cumberland, RI (US); **Douglas A Schultheis**, Cumberland, RI (US); **Mark Foster**, Cumberland, RI (US)

(73) Assignee: **Hasbro, Inc.**, Pawtucket, RI (US)

(*) Notice: Subject to any disclaimer, the term of this patent is extended or adjusted under 35 U.S.C. 154(b) by 730 days.

(21) Appl. No.: **11/742,985**

(22) Filed: **May 1, 2007**

(51) **Int. Cl.**
A63H 18/00 (2006.01)
(52) **U.S. Cl.** **446/444**; 446/236; 446/168
(58) **Field of Classification Search** 446/236, 446/444, 332, 429, 168–171
See application file for complete search history.

(56) **References Cited**

U.S. PATENT DOCUMENTS

1,524,615 A	*	1/1925	Diederichs	.... 446/332
1,704,012 A	*	3/1929	Marx	.... 446/332
1,778,038 A	*	10/1930	Parke	.... 446/332
2,066,239 A	*	12/1936	Tahsler	.... 446/236
2,602,262 A	*	7/1952	Nichols	.... 446/445
3,514,108 A	*	5/1970	Sidney et al.	.... 463/68
3,531,119 A	*	9/1970	Bonanno	.... 463/68
3,948,520 A	*	4/1976	Barlow	.... 463/68
4,041,873 A		8/1977	Jones	
4,209,935 A	*	7/1980	Parker	.... 463/64
4,237,648 A	*	12/1980	Moe et al.	.... 446/332
4,395,041 A		7/1983	Goldfarb et al.	
5,376,037 A	*	12/1994	Finkbeiner	.... 446/236
5,452,893 A	*	9/1995	Faulk et al.	.... 446/444
5,657,856 A	*	8/1997	von Froreich	.... 198/817
5,791,253 A		8/1998	Schultheis et al.	

* cited by examiner

Primary Examiner — Alvin A Hunter
Assistant Examiner — Urszula M Cegielnik
(74) *Attorney, Agent, or Firm* — Perry Hoffman

(57) **ABSTRACT**

An entertainment apparatus and methods propelling toy vehicles about multiple tracks providing a variety of play modes while mechanically driven by a single motor and simple belt sub-system. A motor and a plurality of adjacent discs disposed in the same horizontal plane are mechanically engaged with the motor for rotating the discs simultaneously in the same direction. An object alternately engages each of the plurality of discs and at least one transition area is adjacent the plurality of discs and disposed in the same horizontal plane for facilitating the action of the object about the plurality of discs. One or more objects are propelled about one or more tracks providing a variety of play modes.

18 Claims, 11 Drawing Sheets

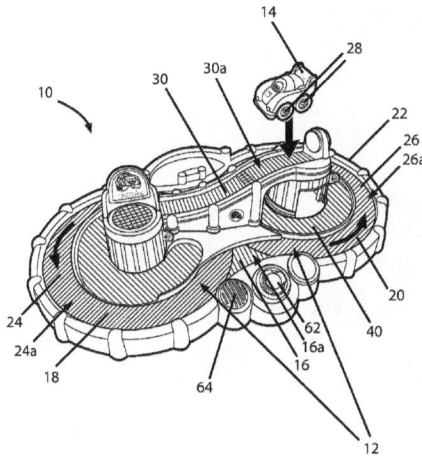

US00D451524B1

(12) **United States Design Patent** (10) Patent No.: **US D451,524 S**

Morris (45) Date of Patent: ** Dec. 4, 2001

(54) **EXTRUDER FOR MODELING COMPOUND**

(75) Inventor: **Lamont Curtis Morris**, Hope, RI (US)

(73) Assignee: **Hasbro, Inc.**, Pawtucket, RI (US)

(**) Term: **14 Years**

(21) Appl. No.: **29/136,333**

(22) Filed: **Jan. 26, 2001**

(51) **LOC (7) Cl.** **15-04**
(52) **U.S. Cl.** **D15/135**; D21/528
(58) **Field of Search** D12/528, 468;
D15/135, 136; 425/DIG. 57, 154, 207,
376.1, 381; 446/20, 491

(56) **References Cited**

U.S. PATENT DOCUMENTS

D. 268,043 * 2/1983 Orenstein D21/528

* cited by examiner

Primary Examiner—Antoine Duval Davis
(74) Attorney, Agent, or Firm—Kurt R. Benson

(57) **CLAIM**

The ornamental design for a extruder for modeling compound, as shown.

DESCRIPTION

FIG. 1 is a perspective view of the extruder for modeling compound of the instant invention;

FIG. 2 is a front elevational view thereof;

FIG. 3 is a rear elevational view thereof;

FIG. 4 is a top plan view thereof;

FIG. 5 is a bottom plan view thereof;

FIG. 6 is a left side elevational view thereof; and,

FIG. 7 is a right side elevational view thereof.

1 Claim, 7 Drawing Sheets

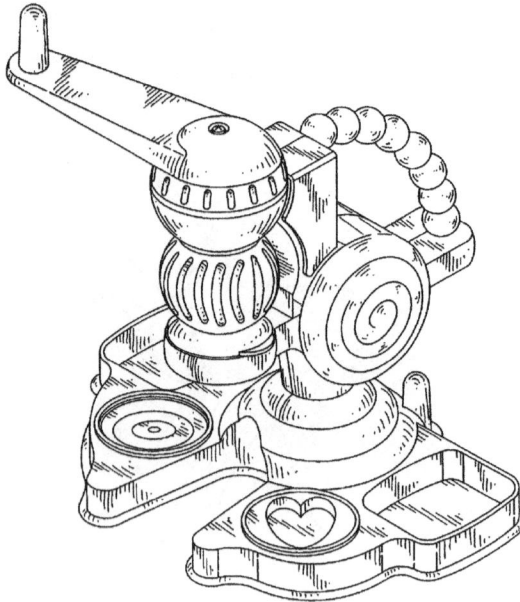

(12) **United States Design Patent** (10) Patent No.: **US D500,528 S**

Morris et al. (45) **Date of Patent:** ** **Jan. 4, 2005**

(54) **LIGHT BOX**

(75) Inventors: **LaMont Curtis Morris**, Cumberland, RI (US); **Paul Weingard**, Rehoboth, MA (US)

(73) Assignee: **Hasbro, Inc.**, Pawtucket, RI (US)

(**) Term: **14 Years**

(21) Appl. No.: **29/198,257**

(22) Filed: **Jan. 27, 2004**

(51) LOC (7) Cl. **21-01**
(52) U.S. Cl. **D21/324**; D26/37; D21/333
(58) Field of Search .... D21/324, 328, D21/333; D26/1, 37–50, 113; 273/148 B; 463/1, 29–35, 46, 47; 362/154, 127, 181, 183, 200, 208, 362, 800, 806

(56) **References Cited**

U.S. PATENT DOCUMENTS

2,575,269 A	11/1951	Hall
3,067,536 A	12/1962	Brittsan
3,530,615 A	9/1970	Meyer
3,568,357 A	3/1971	Lebensfeld
3,716,936 A	2/1973	Miller
4,196,539 A	4/1980	Speers
4,350,070 A *	9/1982	Bahu 84/612
4,550,916 A	11/1985	Ortiz
4,891,030 A	1/1990	Gertzfeld
5,217,295 A *	6/1993	Tortola et al. 362/109

5,324,224 A	6/1994	Anderson et al.
5,391,105 A	2/1995	Jones
5,555,163 A	9/1996	Pisani
D375,515 S *	11/1996	Takeda et al. D17/99
5,661,632 A *	8/1997	Register 361/683
5,672,108 A *	9/1997	Lam et al. 463/39
5,876,262 A	3/1999	Kelly et al.
D439,351 S *	3/2001	Kiba et al. D26/37
D460,495 S *	7/2002	Naghi et al. D21/333
D467,979 S *	12/2002	Lee D21/333
D468,037 S	12/2002	Jarvis
D472,937 S *	4/2003	Chang D21/333
D495,013 S *	8/2004	Hussaini et al. D21/324

* cited by examiner

Primary Examiner—Prabhakar Deshmukh
(74) *Attorney, Agent, or Firm*—Michael Best & Friedrich LLP

(57) **CLAIM**

The ornamental design for a light box, as shown.

DESCRIPTION

FIG. 1 is a perspective view of the light box of the instant invention;
FIG. 2 is a top plan view thereof;
FIG. 3 is a bottom plan view thereof;
FIG. 4 is a front elevational view thereof;
FIG. 5 is a rear elevational view thereof;
FIG. 6 is a right elevational view thereof; and,
FIG. 7 is a left side elevational view thereof.

1 Claim, 5 Drawing Sheets

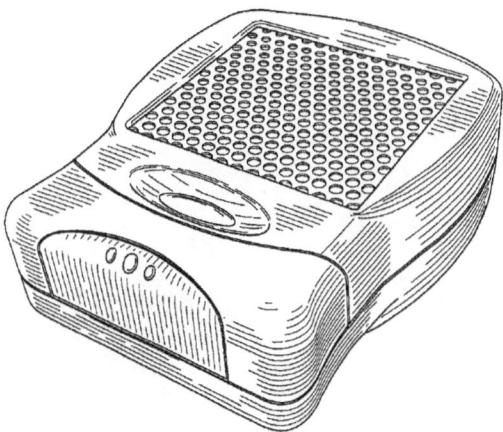

United States Patent [19]

Morris et al.

[11] Patent Number: 4,929,216

[45] Date of Patent: May 29, 1990

[54] ROTATING RING AND CHARACTER TOY

[75] Inventors: Lamont C. Morris, Chicago; Wayne A. Kuna, River Forest; Rouben T. Terzian, Chicago, all of Ill.

[73] Assignee: Marvin Glass & Associates, Chicago, Ill.

[21] Appl. No.: 255,763

[22] Filed: Oct. 11, 1988

[51] Int. Cl.5 .... A63H 11/08; A63H 29/08; A63H 5/00; A63H 17/26

[52] U.S. Cl. .... 446/324; 446/169; 446/272; 446/280; 446/449; 273/128 A

[58] Field of Search .... 446/169, 168, 171, 173, 446/233, 234, 236, 237, 238, 268, 269, 272, 274, 275, 279, 280, 288, 396, 437, 431, 450, 451, 324, 325, 326, 435, 449, 409, 411; 273/424, 425, 428, 128 A, 126 R, 126 A

[56] References Cited

U.S. PATENT DOCUMENTS

2,232,244	2/1941	Kiefer	446/269
2,351,762	6/1944	Hoover	446/269
2,400,981	5/1946	Dishmaker	446/449
2,747,328	5/1956	Zalkind	446/411 X
2,937,475	5/1960	Crawford	446/409 X
3,475,855	11/1969	Edwards	446/431
3,571,970	3/1971	Dunn	446/451
3,682,477	8/1972	Harkins	446/237 X
3,825,263	7/1974	Santangelo	273/425 X
4,203,251	5/1980	Malek et al.	446/236
4,610,637	9/1986	Ferguson	446/451 X

FOREIGN PATENT DOCUMENTS

20674	9/1955	Fed. Rep. of Germany	446/279
8907	9/1956	Fed. Rep. of Germany	446/322
607501	7/1926	France	446/450
2128097	4/1984	United Kingdom	446/280

Primary Examiner—Robert A. Hafer
Assistant Examiner—D. Neal Muir
Attorney, Agent, or Firm—John S. Pacocha

[57] ABSTRACT

A cylindrical ring and a character having a number of extending parts that are circumscribed by a circle having a diameter equal to the inside diameter of the ring are readily combinable by a child to make a rotating toy. Insertion and removal of the character from the inside of the ring are facilitated by making the ring of a deformable material. The combined ring and character are placed in a vehicle in contact with the vehicle wheels so that as the vehicle is moved along a playing surface, the wheels rotate the combined ring and character. Part of the vehicle body is hinged for closing an opening through which the combined ring and character are inserted. Above the ring is a transparent dome in which a ball is positioned in contact with the ring so that as the combined ring and character rotate, the ball rotates within the dome. Other accessories provide rotatable surfaces which engage the outer curved surface of the cylindrical ring to rotate the combined ring and character. Yet another accessory provides surfaces on which the combined ring and character roll, under the force of gravity, and produce a bell ringing action.

16 Claims, 2 Drawing Sheets

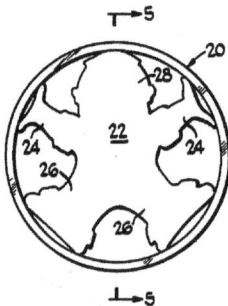

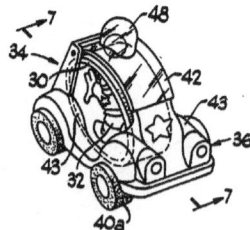

www.ingramcontent.com/pod-product-compliance
Lightning Source LLC
Chambersburg PA
CBHW020904090426
42736CB00008B/487